THE VINEYARD ABOVE THE SEA

CHARLES TOMLINSON

THE VINEYARD ABOVE THE SEA

OxfordPoets
CARCANET

First published in 1999 by
Carcanet Press Limited
4th Floor, Conavon Court
12–16 Blackfriars Street
Manchester M3 5BQ

A CIP catalogue record for this book
is available from the British Library
ISBN 1 903039 01 0

The publisher acknowledges financial assistance
from the Arts Council of England

Set in 10pt Bembo by Bryan Williamson, Frome
Printed and bound in England by SRP Ltd, Exeter

To Brenda

Acknowledgements

Acknowledgements are due to the editors of the following: *Agenda, The American Poetry Review, The Critical Quarterly, The New Criterion, New Writing, Paris Review, Partisan Review, Poetry Nation, Rosa Cubica, Sibila, La Stampa, Southwest Review, The Times Literary Supplement, Vuelta*. These poems first appeared in *The Hudson Review*: 'Directions', 'The Tree House', 'Gibbet', 'The Vineyard Above the Sea', 'Fonte Gaia'.

Contents

The pause at the turn, however infinitesimal,
    Is there to ensure we do not run ahead
Of the heartbeat, the knowledge in the blood
    That will not be hurried beyond a present good
Before it has fed on it. Where are you going
    And towards what beyond, asks the pulsation
To which everything is bound: time to return
    To the paced-out path for those who raced it.

A Festivity
for Fred Siegel

Late afternoon and a rumble of planes,
    Flight-lanes imprinted on the sky
In crumbling chalk, decaying arabesques;
    Or leaning a Jacob's ladder up between
One midair plateau and the next above it.
    Pluming away, they start to congregate
With that which they most resemble now –
    The passing nebulous cloud company
That crowd before a disappearing sun
    And still are on display, once it has gone,
In the light it has left them, a yellow band
    Like the sand of some celestial beach
Which is gradually becoming sea, and they
    A blackening armada trailing smoke.
Dark shipshapes, spectres of voyaging,
    Keep moving on like the planes themselves
That are creating, as they go, their own unspooling
    Tickertaped west, leaving us ours,
An abandoned festivity to be completed
    Elsewhere, a few wraiths suspended wavering,
Catching the red rising from below,
    Above an embered twilight that in cold
And dark is alchemising to an airy streak of sunset gold.

Mythology

The Greeks must have got it from clouds. Polypheme
    Cranes up bull-necked over the horizon
And scans sky above the valley. The shape
    That threatens him, all muscles, moving domes,
Body or city rising compact,
    Must be a god in the making – higher
Than him in fact. He goes on growing
    Gazing: the vertical white nude
Grows, too, and spreads its snows
    Overhead, as if it would outdo
Any aggressor from below. He pauses, now.
    His one eye must clearly have seen
How the immaculate upward drift is beginning
    To fray from its perfect outline
And slowly grey against the blue behind it,
    Letting it through unawares as it stretches and thins,
Scarcely distinguishable at the edges
    From that azure suffusion that seeps in
Little by little, drinking the god whole.
    Olympus is overthrown. Its battlements
Are coming down. An anchorless ship,
    It is changing into the mist surrounding it,
And the thunder sounds its undoing wide
    As it gigantically, visibly drowns
And watching Polypheme crouches there satisfied.

In Abruzzo

The stretched-out sleepers, limestone sentinels
        Who have forgotten what camp it is
They are defending, do not realise
        That other eyes are overlooking their shoulders –
The Great Rock, the range of the Maiella –
        Heaped-up, crowding one another back
In this history of shift and slide, of sudden
        Fissuring along the mountainside
Into the worked stone world of dwelling
        (You might seize on the wrought iron
Of its balconies as the façade folds open
        And crumbles down). Today the distances
Are at truce, nothing toeing loose
        The long negotiation between flesh and stone:
Beneath ramparts, the awning stripes
        Of a market give back the light,
And voices, climbing up from below
        Tell human time and not the cold
Chronology of looming strata. But the slow
        Ranges of silently invading cloud
This July day of mountain autumn
        Begin to unsay the promises of sun
That opens a path through the pale reaped hayfields,
        Warming this parapet we are leaning on.

Trebiano

'I live in a small city, and I prefer
to dwell there that it may not become smaller still.' (Plutarch)

I

These outposts were the centres once.
    The bulwarks of the ruined fort contain
The village cistern. What you find
    Are veering streets stacked above a plain
So wide that you scan its flat immensity
    For sails. You can hear more than you see
Down there, the clang and ricochet
    Of the place to which activity has fled
Flung up at you, and to be heard
    Even in the gullies between the dwellings
And against the walls of the bishop's house
    From which its inhabitant departed
Centuries since. What Trebiano lacks
    Is its Plutarch perhaps to come – the single
Mind that will expand the circuit of that site
    On which the hill-top houses stand
Sending down pin-prick morse
    From shuttered windows into Ligurian night.

Hawks
Inhabit the gaps in castle masonry.
Stones that hold down the rooftiles here
Come from its crumbled wall whose ivy
Forces a slow and silent entry
Gripping and grinding the stone's precariousness.
Imprinting themselves on the summit silences,
Rumours of cars crossing the valley floor.
A fig-tree has fastened itself to the threshold where
A wind is rising with tidal sounds through the leaves.
Thwack of the returning hawk that lands in its lair.

III

Bent above distances at this high window,
    Crow's nest that does not sway surveying change:
The plain of the Magra crossed, re-crossed by rain
    Yields for an instant to a far suggestion
Of sun that coldly catches the blades –
    Two sickle-shapes where the river curves
Then curves again winding to the Tyrrhenian
    Which shows, a sliver of sea, blotted by hills
(The eye drawn right) that mass, ripple and then fall
    In leisurely sloping folds of green
To where the land ends and the Ligurian sea
    Extends water once more in horizontal calm.
The linear glint goes out as the rain
    Shadows it over, the two half-moon blades
Darken beneath the flying fringes
    That advance below and have already reached
The dorsal roof-ridges of this village,
    Tile locked on tile, like the bones
Of an extinct species. Rain
    Glitters and slides into gutters polishing
The cheerless ancient houses that cling
    In two parallel streets to a hillside
More precipice than slope. We are that continuing race
    Defying the attempts of earth itself
To have done and huddle us off it. We
    Persist like the returning light that, overcome,
Reaches out to touch the surfaces it had lost,
    As if it were resurrected from under a sea
Off a phosphorescence as marine-sharp, nacreous,
    As that which enamels these now shimmering roofs.

The Vineyard Above the Sea

This frontal hill falls sheer to water,
    Rugged forehead whose rhythmic folds
Are of stone, not flesh – walls
    That hold up the soil and the vines between,
Whose final fruit, essence and asperity,
    Is wine like daylight, tasting of the sea.
I lift a glass of it towards the sun
    Catching, within, the forms essentialised
Of these cliff-edge vine-rows –
    Cables hoisting a harvest to the summit –
And beyond the ripple of rock-shoulders
    Bearing the load of grapes and stone,
The town itself – almost a woman's name –
    Corniglia, as tight-gripped to its headland
As to their heights these walls, floating
    Along the contours like the recollection
Of a subsided ocean that has left behind
    The print of waves. Windows, doors
In the heaped façades cast a maternal glance
    Over a geology festooned, transformed,
Where through the centuries it hunched a way
    Towards these cube-crystals of the houses,
This saline precipice, this glass of light.

Fonte Gaia

Children beg *monetine*
and fling them — *per la fortuna!* —
into the waters of the fountain.
A pigeon perched on her head,
Sapienza, not Fortuna
governs this flow,
graceful and severe.
Between what they wish for and what they will know
let no malignity interfere,
no waters tainted by coins and excrement
infect and blur the intent
innocence of their trust in luck.

News

The people in the park
are not news:
they only go to prove
what everyone knows –
the sufficiency
of water and a few trees.

The people in the gallery
are not news either:
they are here for more trees
and the permanence of water
of various kinds: everything
from the seastorm to spring rain.

Walking in the street,
we are not news, you and I,
nor is the street itself
in the first morning sun
which travels to us from so far out
sharpening each corner with its recognition.

News
wilting underfoot, news
always about to lose its savour,
the trees arch over the blown sheets
rain is reducing to a transparent blur
as if water with trees were alpha and omega.

Oporto

I

And then the river
overflowed and rose
uphill through
the long canals of streets:
it mistook
the churches for cliffs
and the chapels within
for sea-caves
and covered them
with an armour
of golden molluscs.

II

Is this a queen
or is it the queen
of heaven balancing
her gigantic crown
like the burdens
the peasant women
carry on their heads?

III

Luke, with a quill in hand,
is concentrating:
at his feet, the eagle
brings his inkwell to him
strapped round its neck,
and gazes up towards
the gospel he is penning.

IV

In a glass case
the wrapped dead Christ
in a covering like butchers' muslin
bordered with lace.

V

A female saint,
with a shepherd's crook,
holds on her left hand
an open book,
a dove craning up out of it.

VI

Leaving
I drop coins
into the begging bowl
of cupped
unclean fingers
and though we greet
by touch
our eyes do not meet.

Rua do Carriçal

The inhabitants of Rua do Carriçal,
in their island street –
their urban Innisfree
jammed between two thoroughfares –
live remote from either
psychosis or a nunnery, and yet
someone has written on the wall
Psychotic Lesbian Nuns.
The woman washing her balcony floor
cannot read this scrawl
since it is daubed in English,
but wrings out her rag
in island innocence. Her neighbour
has trained his vines
to an iron trellis and emerges
from the greenery below
watering a miniature garden –
strawberries in plastic tubs, a slim
rectangle of soil in which
cabbage and cala lilies grow
side by side, gigantic roses
looming above lettuces,
striped pumpkin and potatoes.
Besieged by pylons,
a radio-mast, street-
end traffic and the monomaniac note
from a generator,
its parked cars
cluster as close as pumpkins growing,
where, immune from harm,
the pre-Freudian Carriçal exudes
into Lusitanian noon
its convent calm.

The Green Balloon

In Citadel Park,
the stalled balloon refuses
to climb across the trees
and from there take in
the rowers on the lake below,
all pulling away in time
with the accordion music:
the combusting of its gas,
loud as a school of drummers,
seems vanity and excess,
where every child
is attached to its own
floating toy balloon
that effortlessly discovers
the most convenient current
to keep it hovering in air.
Those cooped in their basket on the ground
might well have found out
children and rowers with a single
swoop of the eye up there
and, between the two,
the human pyramid
the club of athletes
is erecting into view,
storey rising on storey
of the firm yet slightly
trembling arms, building
to a summit that a child
ascends. Arriving at the top,
he turns and takes a bow
as applause breaks below him.
The pyramid then undoes itself,
with pauses for more applause,
as the levels come faultlessly apart
and back to earth. But in all this
accumulation and deconstruction,
the balloon at the park gates
still hesitates to rise
more than a few feet, and then

laboriously returns to earth again
like a bounced ball
gigantic in slow motion.
Its hydrocephalic mass,
doubled by a bobbing shadow,
nods at a gesturing statue
that appears to be fending it off.
Its mountainous shade,
dragging beside its own
lighter-than-air, great
inflated, bottle-green bag,
hangs, half shadow
of a doubt, half threat.

Barcelona

Hellas

1. KÉA

It begins with its lighthouse, ends with a tapering down –
    No town, no jetty – of rock into water:
In between – houses, a few, set back
    On barren heights, crossed only
By the frayed rope of a wandering wall
    That negotiates slope and drop to disappear
Then finally show itself on top
    Of the highest point. What does it contain?
Here, neither sheep nor crop. Who is it clings
    Still to Kéa in those scattered dwellings?
We are sliding past, watching this apparition
    Fade into the blaze of Aegean noon.

2. APOLLO AT DELPHI

Darkness – as if it were the shadow of a cloud
   The wind was hurrying away – slides
Visibly off the plain, already sails
   Up the grey sides of the mountain to the peak
And leaves its high stones naked as Apollo.

3. EPIDAUROS

Into the circle of the theatre
at Epidauros, faced
by its absent auditors
ten thousand strong, I launch
through acoustic space
the ship I have most in mind –
Hopkins' Deutschland – and can hear
(his verses, thewed
like an Attic ode)
syllabic echoes cut into the atmosphere
climbing on ancient feet
the limestone tiers
where listening cyclamen have pushed their way
between the slabs
up out of Hades.

4. FRAGMENT

Water, a faint aural thread,
that once fed the fountain.
After invasion, turmoils, time,
the place, like the poems of Sappho,
all shards, shreds.

The wren, the lizard and the cicada,
left in possession of the ground,
do not try to imagine
what is no longer there nor ask
which god sanctuaried here,
how did his music sound,
who is this headless woman
draped in a stone snake?

5. OLYMPIA
    in dispraise of ruins

That intelligent lizard
knows more of the place than I do. To him
all this is a city still complete,
its every fissure leads
into sunlit avenue, shadowy retreat.
I approve of his ignorance of archaeology:
I, too, cannot read a ruin with ease.
For him, of course, the question does not arise.
What Greece lacks is buildings that are entire.
Not those drab towns or these chipped remains,
It is architecture that I admire.
A true building builds you up as you look at it.
The pleasures of ruins are not infinite.

6. PASTORAL

Goats in Arcadia
tintinnabulate still,
emerge from the milking shed
at the field's margin
with a crash of bells
and hurl themselves downhill
in a cavalry charge.

Goatherd regroups them,
not with a dog or threats,
but with low conch sounds
blown out of the hollow
of his cupped hands,

and through the sloping paddock,
in file they follow the man
in shirt, jeans, slouch hat,
unpied piper, reincarnate Pan.

7. LIKE GREEK PROSE

                      'Like Greek prose
with its passion for balance and antithesis,
elaborated by every kind of parallelism
including rhyme.' That might well be
a definition for the kind of poetry
that runs the spoken word
hard into the foreseeable and the unforeseen,
into patterns that lie
at the edges of what is stated, rhyme
suddenly knotted and related
to what was apparently done and gone,
and now, in perfected balance, moves
however unsymmetrically, with the dance
of forces, on and below those surfaces
which are the poem. And take this scene.
A Lapith is overcoming a Centaur:
with effort and yet balletic ease it bends
and accommodates it to this frieze, a half-
rhyme in the question and answer of their posture.
That, too, is poetry, that, too, is Greek.

8. FROM THE GREEK

Distances, Alexander hungered across these.
Words, the commonwealth of Socrates.
Honey, the monomania of bees.

9.   IN THE CATHEDRAL

The Archbishop was preaching that Sunday.
My ear could distill
thanatos, thanatos
out of the torrent of the unintelligible.
Whatever his meaning, his tone was clear:
he had not come here to flatter.
When he got down and was distributing the bread,
holding out a hand to be kissed,
I saw what I had missed before –
the painted image
of a small sad god
spread out on his rood
and the congregation
was clutching bits of bread
pausing to kiss the silver ikons
on their way out:
thanatos, thanatos
was sleeping now, the fray
with a vengeful deity over and done,
as the tide of the after-service conversation
rose and spread across the beach of Sunday afternoon.

10. MELVILLE ON THE ACROPOLIS

Not magnitude, not lavishness
But form, the site.
> (Herman Melville)

for Vincent Scully

He scanned the hill-top temple and the spread
   Horizon of both ocean and of land
With a sailor's eye. Not the dark
   Flux of unending sea – the form
Was Doric and the site lay clear,
   The whole of distance swung in a single arc.
The temple was the containing vantage, he
   The temple's eye left hungry by the sea:
Here, depth rode steady, distances
   Must answer to the pull and measure
Of the ruined, sunlit colonnade that still
   Culminated the upward forces of its hill.
The form, the site: one held in the other's bowl –
   Stone against space, space opening onto mountain –
And the mariner balanced precariously whole
   On this stone ship headed towards Hymettos.

11. HOMECOMING

Frost-fur on every gate and fence:
where the sunlight reaches late,
grey shadows beneath beech and oak
across whitened grass;
but a ticking, a trickling of melted drops
from branches onto leaves long down
and sodden now
where, a steadily climbing vapour,
rime filters back into the atmosphere,
into the invisibility
that clothes all gods.

On the Dunes

for Richard Verrall

The dunes are blue in the eye of the sea,
Swayed into changes that might well be
Sea in themselves. For the sea, no wrecks exist.
They are merely the emanations of the mist
That sink into obliviousness to be caressed,
Processed like these sands, till what remains
Are monuments merely to the sea's power,
Sunk palaces through which the fish are free to display
Their malleability and their scales – also like the sea
When the waves agree to be calm like dunes
Building, changing silently, the one real
Challenge to all that equilibrium,
The tilt of the horizon, that is bringing to bear
The only other eye the sea must fear – the sky –
If it is still to retain its halcyon mood,
Its mine of unadulterated blue,
And not negotiate with the colour of the dunes,
When there is sand in the teeth of the wave
And what is real is not to be sluiced away
And the shreds of dead fish and of men
Assert their right to be recognised
For what they were before the omniverous water
Washed them down with its midnight feast,
And then a congratulatory sun offered
To reduce what was still floating pulverised.
Beyond, the dunes had watched it all
And wait now to reinstate themselves,
And the winds that had torn up the cosmic fence
Resolve on coexistence, sea beside sand, silence.

Here where the certainty of land begins,
The ocean writes and rewrites its margins:
You can read along the rippling of the sand
The script advancing in its cursive hand,
Denying it has ever signed before
The dozen dishonoured treaties of this shore –
The harbours disappearing into silt,
Alexandra's cottage – royal Edward's guilt
Cost her less smart there – level with the tide.
To the hopes of merchant or of monarch's bride
The ocean does not deal long satisfactions,
Deep in its own ungovernable transactions.
White on this inland table lies a shell.
Lift it towards your ear and listen well.
The approaching breath of ocean that you hear
Says that the world won't end in ice or fire,
But lost to the tidal trickeries of water.

Directions

Just when you're sure that you're not getting near,
A tunnel of trees will suddenly appear
To undo doubt. You enter its half-light.
A mile more now and you will be in sight
Of a long, low house – that's ours. The tunnel, first –
A spot authority will one day worst
Because of its lack of 'visibility'
That helps us sense far more than we can see.
My one regret's that you arrive by car
And not by boat; that these few metres are
Asphalt, not winding water – how this road
Would flow in majesty, a river–god,
If that were the case; then, this shuttered shade
Would filter the daylight through the dark it's made
To sparkle off the surface round your prow,
As off the chromium and paintwork now
Heaving into view. Already I
Can hear the gear change, as you leave the high
Ground for the low that we inhabit here,
Beside the dampness of a genuine river.
You have arrived. You need seek no further.

In the Room

The room is submerged under restless waters –
the floating shadows of the birches
swimming in sunlight through the sable shade
where armchairs and a table
have taken root within four walls:
at each fresh onrush of the wind
the tree limbs and the leaves out there
renew their quivering race across a floor
where distance has come indoors
to reclaim the angled confine for the season
dancing it back to space.

The Gift

The allée I call it. It is scarcely that
    For all the gallic geometry of trunks
Facing each other along either side
    Of a straight, receding track. Call it
English and accidental, two hedges
    Outgrowing their purposes, to meet
Overhead in arched and tangled boughs,
    An invitation to pace the shadows
Imagining a verse-line to accommodate
    The play of muscle in the sway of walking,
Linearity plucked at by leaf and light.
    And yet – it is not quite English, either:
You have only to scratch this county and
    Up come the oyster shells and tegulae
Of Rome. No need for archaeology to identify
    Roads like these that have lost their way
In the long recessions of empire. Call
    This one an imperial gift that Caesar
Scarcely intended leaving here
    In the far fold of this valley, shaded
By upstart Cotswold post-colonial trees.

Poem

The great cloud-barrier, building
    At sunset above the skyline, hides
The sun itself, lit by a tinge of fire
    Along its topmost reaches – high ground,
A frontier to the land below, an illusion
    That we live bounded by foot-hills,
In touch with mountains soon to appear
    Out of the hills themselves which go on growing
Above us, cancelling the horizon here.
    So we, too, are within reach of summits,
Our valley a scooped-out shelter
    Under their bulk. And this illusion
Holds us like a solid thing, as firm
    As a poem in its imagining step by step
A world into being that is not there –
    Then is, until that fallen fire begins
To penetrate in a glow the vertical mass
    And whole ingots now show through
Suffusing it as the molten fragments
    Drop behind the curvature of space
Leaving the would-be climber of that hill
    Standing earthbound in the chill of evening.
Cries from the first owl, the shrill fox
    Screaming for a mate, soon leave him
In the irrefutable cold, to the world's slow turning
    Beneath the light of a gradually appearing moon.

For Want of Seraphim

A plane (half-heard)
is pulling out a thread
on the blue of afternoon:
the winter sun
embers horizon clouds
that one by one
submit themselves to dark –
a deeper blue
than that on which the thread
is spreading upwards now
catching a glow of gold
from the low hidden orb:
so why should heaven be poor
for want of seraphim where this
thin gold thread
goes on unroving
in mythless apotheosis
above the dead and living?

Measure

Crossing the field
I catch a wandering light
on the road above it –
a car that veers
and disappears and then
like a lantern
swung from side to side,
from dark to light,
shapes out the twisted distances
the road loops through
before taking aim as an arrow might to flow
straight out of darkness:
I watch it go
this lantern of a car
restored to the linear,
to the visible roadbed
and taking the measure of what lies ahead.

Wall

I

The builders of the wall have pitched a tent,
A single sheet to keep them from the rain.
They have an entire field to circumvent
With the woodland next to it, and seen from here
What they are building looks more like a ship:
Effortlessly it might bear them down
Across the Cotswold troughs and to that gate
Where spring awaits them and their voyage ends.
The tin-can rap trails from their radio
To shorten the long way they have to go
Even under sail. Today the ice
Grips stone to stone. A little noonday sun
May gently prise them open later on.
But no one is saying so, or laying bets.
The boat is grounded and the two man crew
Gaze back on what they do not need to do:
Now comes the wait, the cold, the cigarettes.

The two man crew — look, one of them's a girl,
Her tow hair all the hat she deigns to wear
In the February freeze. Ungauntleted
Her carmined finger-ends claw rigid stone
She turns into a wall. 'Seven years,' she says,
When I ask her how long she has worked like this.
Against the blue, a high transparent moon
Leads in the month above an afternoon
Already darkening. How many years
Went to the making of as many walls
As contour out these valleys, half of them
Ruinous like this one when she started?
Silently the moon computes them all
And adds a gradual shadow to each wall
Including hers. And do her hands at night
Feel for those frosty surfaces the moonlight
Turns diamantine? I think her sleep,
The easy conscience of a youthful body,
Where time so far has seized no hostages,
Is undug limestone, spring-fed, bedded deep.

III

Came snow by night, as silent as a thief,
With slow addition, with solicitude
And definition not to be seen until
The morning dawns on new-found surfaces
The fall has brought to light: facets of a hill
Climb into sight and fill the emptiness
Of space ungauged. The builders gone, the whole
Builds itself back into receding white
Where distances and nearness now unite
In one clear structure quarried into time.
The snow-coped wall winds from its summit down
In each direction, like an ample wing,
Flying and yet feeling for the ground,
A gesture it required four hands to make
That snow and limestone link without a break.

Snowbound

for Jordi and Nuria

Now we have locked the doors against the snow
And feel it falling at each curtained window,
The house walls seem to thicken and resist
That movement into flocculence and mist,
Shapes that take the impression of the winds,
Scarving themselves around the gable-ends,
Or piling white oblivion on the stones
That once were ways, alternatives, directions
Refusing to become what they are now –
The unmapped territories of the falling snow.
But the room looms squarer as the tightening cold
Penetrates the fault-lines of our threshold:
Here, whiteness of the open book withstands
These long advances out of polar lands
To claim all for the north, that cannot find –
A roving presence, pathless, angered, blind –
The grain this hate of harvest would efface,
Our cell of fire beneath the blank of space.

Pallor of blossom between still-gaunt trees:
The blackthorn's white acetylene is clearing
Spaces for summer and the vast arrival,
Swimming whose floodtide we shall still recall
This first and tentative, this weightless stirring
Of whiteness above the thicket of winter's vestiges.

I place on the sill a saucer
that I fill with water:
it rocks with a tidal motion,
as if that porcelain round
contained a small sea:
this threshold ocean
throws into confusion
the image that it seizes
out of the sky – the moon
just risen, and now in pieces
beneath the window: the glass
takes in the image at its source,
a clear shard of newness,
and lets it into the house
from pane to pane
riding slowly past:
when I look again
towards the sill, its dish
of moonlight is recomposing:
it lies still, from side to side
of the ceramic circle
curving across the water,
a sleeping bride:
for the moon's sake
do not wake her,
do not shake the saucer.

Storm Song

Rain, targeting the pool,
a blink, as the first grain of it
hits and disappears
into the bullseye it has made:
a circle expands and vanishes
towards the water's edge:
wheels within wheels
rim round into infinity
as rain patterns its way
through a phantasmagoria of similes –
as light at first as the arrival
of summer insects
just glancing at the gelatinous surface,
but by now as insistent
as hammer blows on the restless
metal of swaying water –
not the predictable clockwork tinkle
from Nibelheim, but an enthusiastic
whispering sound of the many hands
that make light work, that make
light of work, effortless, edenic,
and thrumming towards full melody
as the inevitable downpour
solidifies, sings to itself, expands.

The Tree House

Descending the fieldslope,
suddenly one's eyes
catch sight
of the house on the rise beyond
through the boughs of an oak
where it now appears
to be suspended, all
one hundred tons of stone,
its chimneys smoking
out of a warm interior
into a world that looks right
in the cold sunlight
of late-winter afternoon.
They say the King
came here
three hundred years ago
bringing – she called herself
'the Protestant whore' –
Nell Gwyn.
A likely story,
but if it happened
or did not, whoever
occupied that matrimonial bed
lay at the centre of this same
stone enclosure with its smoke
rising, the oak not yet grown
to extend its royal embrace
and make the whole house its own
as it does today
and raise it – a tree house –
up into the air.

The Blossom

I never told you how
I saw one day
in the stream the way
a foam flower grows,
whirled and gathered on
the spindle of an eddy
to a blossom that increased
as the water wound
round it and around,
concentrically piling
foam petals there
in a spawn of eyes,
a rising, whitening
bundle of bubbles
as the onrush and the air
caught in the water's vortex
and hung suspended –
the only thing that did
with the current pouring on
paying, to overcome the one
snag in its liquid line,
this tribute of a flower
absent as the poet says
from all bouquets.

Listening to Leaves

The timbre of the leaves is changing tone –
No more caressive, its metallic hiss,
But scaled and serpentine, setting aside
The bland assurance as of petals swelling
Into massed, harmonious shape and sound.
Behind the hill of leaves, a crag of cloud
Heaves outward into blue, the chartless heights
Borne down above the field's restriction,
Their colour and their cold one single breath
Preluding the autumn and its sequel.
We balance on a blade between the two
Seasons and their sounds that sense must travel through,
Catching from the current of the leaves
Its cross-ply meshing in the weave of time.

Gibbet

This dangling man left hanging in the trees,
Wearing corduroy, check shirt and sack-cloth face,
Who shifts in the current of Atlantic breezes
In the sharpening light, with summer at an end,
Is the scare-crow that the keeper has strung up
From an ash-bough, to protect his fledgling birds,
And jerks into life at every autumn breath,
The guardian of their continuance and their death.

In Winter

The lit-up house is riding like a ship
Anchored below the hill. Owner and owner's wife
Are reading their winter books whose pages fill
Like sails to the breeze of their imaginings –
Different from mine, no doubt, which in the dark
Suppose that by dawn the house might float away,
Leaving its berth as a deserted garden
Surrounded by the neatly labelled saplings
Planted out yesterday. What images
Shake the pheasant already gone to roost
That a late car wakes? Its metallic cry,
A rusty ratchet, grates from the leafless trees
Its stand-and-deliver to all fantasies.

The Sisters

*(Recalling The Westminster Piano Trio:
Shostakovich Opus 67)*

This is not music for the wedding.
The Hasidim are dancing on their graves.
Muted in its highest register,
The cello mourns, and the passacaglia
Paces through one burial the more,
Notes sounding up out of the darkness as
The bare arms circle their instruments
Hacking the downbows, stroke on stroke. How young
They seemed, wielding the weapons of the music,
Burdened by a time they had not lived through,
Yet recognising the lineaments of its sorrow
And the severe exactness art had called them to.

To Modulate

is to discover not invent,
to find a way
that was already there but lay
just out of earshot
awaiting touch,
the sleeper in the wood
who responds, the path
that opens behind you
and beyond: here is the place
you will return to once again
after the alpine ledges, the hurricane
of notes becoming
snow-motes, rain, refreshment,
when all seemed to be
concluded but drew you on,
your footsteps echoing
footsteps gone,
this undulant heard text
that outgoes its own occasion,
when the next time and the next,
what is and was
rears within the ear
its replenished civitas.

The First Death
in memoriam Bruce Chatwin

The hand that reached out from a painted sleeve
    When you sensed that you were dying, gathered you
Into the picture: clothes, furs, pearls,
    Bronze of a vessel, silver of a dish
From which the grapes were overflowing. Tangible
    The minute whiteness of those pearls, the galaxies
They strung; the velvets, sleeves, the welcome
    Among convivial company; the offered hand,
All those glistening appearances that now
    Were to declare the secret of their surfaces –
Surfaces deep as roots. You told
    How you were led at that first death
Through the Venetian plenitude of a room
    Across which a glance confirmed the presence there
Of windows spilling light on this festivity,
    And running beyond them, a silhouette –
The columns of a balustrade – then sky.
    You were let into the anteroom of your heaven
By the eye, moving and attending, finding good
    Those textures it had grazed on like a food.
The second time you died without remission,
    Leaving no report on the lie of the land
Beyond that parapet's stone sill, beyond the gloss
    On all surfaces, rich and indecipherable.

Another Summer

O'Hara admired
'the warm traffic'
(there was less of it then) –
that is my image of him
passing between
two parked cars
and patting the paintwork of one
in affectionate salutation
as if it were a person he already knew.
That was New York in sixty three.
Three more to go.
The month was July when we
lose all apprehension
in the warmth of the world,
our awareness elsewhere
than on personal destiny.
But the place awaited and the hour,
Fire Island offering its sands
to the leisurely attentions of the sea
and the warm traffic of another summer.

To Robert Creeley in
the Judaean Desert

Descending this hill,
we are mending
a broken chain —
those years since we

(again in a desert
place) first met —
by telling over friends
whose lives have ended,

and finding
what remains of our
once world.
There is no

arithmetic can show
a balance struck
between loss and gain,
between now and then.

How high the sky is
here above this
other wilderness
as it was there.

Then

for Frances Partridge

You would lie down, you said, willingly to oblivion then,
As you do each night, knowing no morning would wake you:
You would let the great wave irremediably take you
And deal as it might with the body's floating skein.

What was the resurrection? A dream never to be known.
And centuries have deceived us with its expectations:
Why did we credit the legend-led generations,
With the truth at hand in the gap of each friend gone?

Yet this it is to die – to no longer hear
The clear notes of the cuckoo intersecting
The woodpecker's trills laughingly inflecting
On evening space in the after-rain June air.

In Memoriam Ángel Crespo
(1926-1995)

All things engender shadow –
the rose, the rose-arch and the meadow
sombre among surrounding trees
newly in leaf: shadow
is a continual flow
in the soliloquy we weave
within ourselves, and this
makes the diamond of the day
unreal when it insists
on permanence: but then it takes
a slow and spreading shade
from the contrasting undertone that makes
each facet seem
to both gleam and darken,
changing like the surface of a stream
whose points of light
advancing, dance
on the ripple
pulling them forward
over sunless depth. Listen
and you can hear
at the root of notes
a darker music giving form
to a music already there
filling the innocent ear
with only half its story.

MacDiarmid

The sweetness of the vituperative man
Took me by storm and by surprise –
I'd scarcely looked for courtesies
From one who'd so resisted kith and clan,
But wronged the man I met. Crossing today
A field of thistles in full-scented flower
I think of his note recalling the event
Of meeting then in England, and the way
He signed it in that sloping, suffering hand
Christopher Grieve, and with the pseudonym
Hugh MacDiarmid bracketed beneath,
As if that, too, were memory for him.

History of a House
for Richard and Eileen

The place is surrounded by dancing pines:
    Even their trunks, distorted by the mistral
Bend to one accord. Cleft like a skull,
    It might have been split by lightning,
This house with its cracked wall. A long
    Black aperture divides it, entering
At roof level and running down'
    An entire side. A fanfare
Of Provençal sunlight assails it. Once,
    It had stood firm, bedded on earth
Above the rocks it tried to imitate
    And that mock it now. The sunburst
Serves only to darken its crevices,
    To bring out the blackness in its window eye
Empty of all save shadow and as black
    With vacancy as the crack itself. The pines
In their insouciance do not ask
    Who built it or who lived here;
They dance with the indifference of youth
    At the human years consumed inside.
The lap they dance on and have rooted in
    Proof against mishap, they do not hear
The slow tide rising through the house,
    The electric storm of all the energies
Impounded by that wall, as if it were these
    Had burst the masonry from within.
What happened here is lost to any memory
    Younger than the trees. From the ruined face
Haloed with hints, almost a glance
    Escapes, the lineaments of a persistence
Caught in the climbing light,
    History of a house, occulted and refracted
Between the taciturn rocks and the dance of pines.

By Night

Lights from the hillside farm by night
    Open three doors of fire
Across the swollen stream. It is travelling
    Freighted with the weight a season's rain
Unburdens down all the waterways
    That drain this valley. Those doors
Might well be the entrance to some mine:
    How would you lift its liquid gold,
How would you hold time that is travelling, too,
    In every gleam the light is wakening
Over the waters' face, asleep and flowing
    With its dream of flight towards what end
The winter's night awaits it with? Those strips
    Of flame, vibrant with the current bearing them,
Inscribe our sign and presence here
    Who watch these waters jostling to their fate
In the far-off, sharp sea air –
    Air of origin and end: on the gathered spate
Rides a signature of fire holding its own.